TIGHTENING

the Knot

SUSAN ALEXANDER YATES & ALLISON YATES GASKINS

PIÑON PRESS

P.O. Box 35007, Colorado Springs, Colorado 80935

Library of Congress Catalog Card Number:
95-67771
ISBN 08910-99050

Printed in the United States of America

1 2 3 4 5 6 7 8 9 10/99 98 97 96 95

*To our husbands, John and Will,
with thanksgiving for the joy
of walking through life together.
With you, we know that
"two are better than one,"
and with our God,
we rejoice in the assurance that
"a cord of three strands is not quickly broken"
(from Ecclesiastes 4:9,12).*

Introduction

The shrill ringing of the phone finally woke me. The clock by the bed glowed "2:00 a.m." as I fumbled for the receiver.

"Mom, it's Allison. Get Dad on the phone and wake up my sisters and brothers and tell them to get on the phone too!"

"Are you all right?" I asked, trying to gain consciousness.

"I'm *wonderful*!" She gushed. "Just tell everyone to wake up!"

"But it's the middle of the night," I responded.

"That doesn't matter. *We* have something to tell you all."

We?!

Groggy voices picked up the other phones as Allison and Will exclaimed in unison, "Get up! It's time to start planning a wedding. We just got engaged!"

From that moment on, our lives were thrown into chaos. Details were overwhelming. A wedding dress to choose, groomsmen and bridesmaids to select, the church to reserve, invitations to be sent. It never seemed to end. And the emotions, how they changed! Allison was blinded by excitement, yet at the same time aware that she didn't fully comprehend the reality behind the important step she and Will were taking. Will was eager for the day and already tired of the details of planning. He just wanted to get married. Finally, the day arrived, and with trumpets, flowers, and teary eyes, vows were exchanged.

The wedding ceremony tied the knot. Is this the culmination of our dreams? The final scene of a play with a happy ending?

Or, is it really just the beginning?

We believe that saying "I do" is just the first step. The wedding is like the first day of kindergarten rather than the graduation. It's the beginning of a daily practice of *tightening* the knot, of saying, "I do promise to work on this relationship for the rest of my life."

Sadly, statistics show that a frightening number of marriages are going to fail. Many people marry with unrealistic expectations. Some bring wounds from their own unhappy past. Others have had no positive role models or guidance to help them toward building a marriage that lasts. But no one goes into marriage expecting it to fail. Every couple desperately wants theirs to succeed.

It may have seemed that we were merely planning a wedding, but we knew that we were preparing for a marriage that would last a lifetime. We knew that the relationship is more important than the event.

Even though her mom and dad had been married for nearly twenty-five years and had written books and spoken on building strong families, Allison knew there was more for her to learn. And Susan (Mom), inspired by the young love of the newlyweds, wanted fresh ideas for her own marriage to John. So we decided together to invest some time in learning more about how to build a marriage that lasts.

Allison interviewed over 150 couples with strong marriages, asking them what they did to nurture their relationships. Together we compiled the ideas of friends and the lessons learned from our own experiences.

We have come to understand that there is no perfect marriage, because marriage is the union of two imperfect people. Every couple will experience ups and downs, painful times and joyous ones. We will hurt one another; yet as we forgive, we will grow deeper in our love.

If we take seriously our promise, "Until death do us part," we will need to commit to work on our marriage for the rest of our lives. It can be a fabulous journey! Whether you've been married six months or sixty years, your marriage still needs fresh nurturing.

After Allison and Will had been married about six months, I (Susan) traveled from Virginia to Florida for a visit. Not only was I thrilled with the happiness they exuded, I was challenged by their thoughtfulness toward each other. As I watched them interact, I realized that my daughter was more thoughtful of her husband than I was of John. After twenty-five years of marriage, it's easy to get lazy. I returned home inspired by these newlyweds to work at making my own marriage even stronger.

It is helpful to look back and ask the question, "What really matters in life?" We believe the best answer is *relationships*. Our most fundamental, earthly relationship is that of husband and wife. We hope that this book will encourage you and enrich you as you seek to strengthen the most important tie in your life.

For Both of You

1
Marriage begins when you say "I do."
You have promised to work at this relationship
for the rest of your life.

2
When faced with choices big and small,
ask, "Will this help draw me closer to my mate?"

3
Climb a tree together
and take turns telling stories of your childhood.

4
No one person can love you
as much as you need to be loved. Only God can.
Don't expect your mate to do it all.

5

Write your in-laws and tell them
how much you love their child.

6

Designate a "cuddling chair" or couch in your home.
Take time to cuddle together in it each day.

7

Don't fuss about something you can't change.

8
If your mate goes on a business trip
find out his (or her) address ahead of time
and have a letter waiting for him when he arrives.

9
Don't fear different opinions.
If you agree on everything
one of you isn't necessary.

10

Avoid developing close emotional relationships
with members of the opposite sex.
Instead, draw closer to your mate.

11

When you attend a wedding together, exchange
your rings and silently review your vows together
as the bride and groom say the words.

12
Be the first to say, "I'm sorry." And mean it.

13
Pack a breakfast picnic and watch a sunrise together.

14
Recognize that "how" you each make decisions
may be different.

15
Don't use the words *always* and *never*
when you are in conflict.

16
Put your mate's photo on your desk.
It will remind you of who is first in your life,
and it will make an explicit statement
to your coworkers.

17
When in conflict, begin sentences with
"I feel . . ." instead of "You are. . . ."

18
Think before you act or speak.
Later you may be glad you didn't say or do
what you had intended.

19
Put your mate's towel in the dryer on "hot"
for three minutes and give it to her
as she gets out of the shower on a cold day.

———◈———

20
Hide a note and a chocolate kiss
in your mate's briefcase.

21

Don't box your mate in. People change and your
mate needs you to believe in his or her ability
to grow and change.

22

Surprise your mate by canceling a meeting to spend
time together. A gift of time speaks volumes.

23
Take up a new hobby together.

24
Ask yourself, "What can I do for my mate today
that will be an *unexpected* act of love?" Do it.

25
Phone each other once a day to say,
"Hello, I'm thinking of you."

26

Go out on a date together once a week.
Do this for the rest of your life.

27

Bake chocolate chip cookies or hot pretzels together.

28

Leave a love note on your mate's pillow.

29

Eat dinner together regularly. Switch on
the answering machine, turn off the television,
and eat facing each other.

30

When you're in disagreement, attack the *problems*
together—do not attack each other. Imagine laying
the problem on the table to solve together.

31

Give your mate at least three hugs a day.

32

Don't go to bed angry. Work out what you can.
Make an appointment to talk later. And be forgiving.

33

Notice your mate's talents. Encourage him
or her to develop them and use them.

34

Be an active listener. Repeat to your partner
what you think he or she said.

35

Brag on your partner in front of others.

36

Remember marriage isn't always exciting.
Boredom isn't a sin.

37

Go to a restaurant to have a difficult discussion.
Sit facing each other.

38

Make your mate your best friend.
Share your secrets with him.

39

Make love in a meadow or on a deserted beach.

40

Never say, "Maybe we shouldn't have gotten married."

41

If you are the first one to arrive home in the evening, greet the other with a hug at the door.

42

Assume the best from your mate.

43

Pray together every day. Hold hands and say
the common prayer, known as the Lord's prayer,
which begins, "Our Father, who art in heaven. . . ."

44

Don't keep a record of wrongs done.

45

Avoid sarcasm.

46

Be patient with yourself and with your mate.
You have a lifetime to learn how to be married.

47

Eat dinner by candlelight.

48

Never forget that marriage is the union
of two imperfect people.

49
Keep your promises.

50
Curl up on the couch and spend
an evening looking at old pictures.

51
Sex is a twenty-year warm-up.
It gets better with age and practice.

52
Don't expect your mate to guess
what is on your mind or what you need.
Say it aloud.

53
Develop a mentoring friendship
with an older couple who have a strong marriage.
Ask them for advice and encouragement.

54
Assume that your mate loves you.

55
Consider your mate's concerns
as more important than your own.

56
Don't be devastated by difficulty or hard times.
See them as opportunities for growth.

57
Forget each other's mistakes.

58
Curl up on the couch, turn out all the lights,
light one candle, and share a dessert together.

59
Say "I love you" a lot.

60

Discuss your views on money and plan a yearly budget.

---◈---

61

In your budget include a frivolous category
for each mate to use for something special.

---◈---

62

Ask questions that call for more than
a one-word answer.

63

If your mate snores, buy a sound-masking
(white noise) machine immediately.

64

Learn the things your partner likes,
and study them. For example, golf,
bird watching, art, etc.

65
Don't be discouraged when you discover
you have to work at marriage. Marriage *is* work.

66
When you have a fight remember: Each argument
is a small speck in a lifetime of marriage.

67
Give each other special nicknames, and use them.

68
A good marriage is made when two people
each give 100 percent instead of
50 percent/50 percent.

69
Remember, there is no Prince Charming
and there is no Cinderella.

70

View your differences as blessings. Learn how to
make them work together and compliment
each other rather than cause conflict.

71

Read this book at least once a year,
and add your own ideas
for building a strong marriage.

72

Play music from your young adult years,
and dance the way you did in the "old days."
Encourage your kids to join in.

73

Make sure you hear what your mate is saying.
Ask, "Are you saying this . . . ?"

74

Every day, thank God for something specific in your mate's life. Practice being grateful for each other.

75

Let your mate (and no one else) be the star of your fantasies and imaginations.

76

Take a bubble bath together by candlelight.

77
Let your mate teach you something new.

78
Work together to develop your own holiday traditions.

79
Write your mate a letter and name specific
things you love about him or her.

80
Be on time.

❖

81
Buy a tape of a song you liked when you were dating
and give it with a love note.

❖

82
Give your mate a foot massage.

83

Remember that *how* you say things
is just as important as *what* you say.

84

Bring your mate a present when you return
from a business trip.

85

Make a big deal over your mate's birthday.

86
Rinse your mouth with mouthwash
first thing in the morning.

———◈———

87
Love must be fed to grow.
What can you do today to feed your love?

———◈———

88
Change the bag on the vacuum cleaner.

89

Don't keep mental lists of how your mate has
disappointed you. Keep a list of the ways he
or she has encouraged you.

90

Remember, every marriage is unique because
no two people are alike. Don't expect yours
to be like anyone else's.

91

Save old love letters. Bring them out on a special occasion and read them to each other.

92

Give your mate the benefit of the doubt.

93

Fax love notes to each other at work.

94

Ask yourself: Does my speech and tone reflect condemnation or concern?

95

Occasionally, agree to listen to each other for fifteen minutes apiece, then wait for twenty-four hours to respond to what the other said.

96

Stop whining and start working to make
your marriage stronger.

97

Use problem-solving techniques you've
learned at the office to help in solving
marital conflict.

98
Resist the temptation to withdraw.
Instead take steps toward each other.

99
Do something that makes your mate feel loved.
(It may be different from what makes you feel loved.)

100
Write letters. You can't save phone calls.

101
Show your love for your mate by honoring
his parents and siblings.

102
Guard your tongue. When in doubt,
don't say it until you've thought about it.

103
Don't take things too personally. Develop a light heart.

104

"Absence in love is like water upon fire;
a little quickens, but much extinguishes it."

—HANNAH MORE

105

Buy a book of love poems and read them to each other.

106

Engrave a piece of jewelry with something romantic.

107
Go for a walk in the rain together.

108
Check out an old romantic movie, pop popcorn,
and have a date together at home.

109
Go skinny dipping together.

110
Lie out in the yard, look at stars,
and listen to a concert on tape.

111
Agree to pay off all credit card balances
at the end of each month.

112
Go to church together.

113
Replace your underwear when it wears out.

114
Start a holiday scrapbook together. Record where you were and what you did on each holiday.

115
Give your mate a gift that doesn't cost anything (for instance, a coupon for a back rub).

116

Buy a Christmas ornament together each year
for a special collection.

❖

117

Take your mate's car when he or she
isn't using it, have it washed, and return it
to the same place.

118
Keep a list of interesting things to talk about
when you have time alone together.

———————◈———————

119
Clean up together after a party.
Use the time to discuss the event.

———————◈———————

120
Take lots of silly photos.

121
Remember, if you want your kids to have a strong
marriage they need to see you working on yours.

122
Make a scrapbook of all the special places
you went on dates before you were married.
Give it to your mate as a gift.

123
Go fishing together.

124
Learn how to entertain on a shoestring.
Have "potluck" dinners where each guest
brings food to share.

125
Usher at a concert together. You'll get in free.

126

Take the first fifteen minutes for the two of you
when your mate comes in from work.
Fix a cup of tea and visit.
Tell the kids they can be present but not speak. They'll
soon leave and give you time alone together.

127

Mail letters to your mate at the office.

128
Keep your relationship with your mate first even before the kids. A child's security is increased by knowing that his parents love each other.

129
Go sledding on a snowy golf course in the moonlight.

130
If you can't have separate bathrooms,
have separate toothpaste.

131
Do things to make your mate laugh.
Laughter is a medicine.

132
Take a morning off at home. Stay in bed together.

133
Kiss in the kitchen in front of the children.

134
Recognize that changes—new job, new baby, a move, illness—produce stress in marriage. Take extra time to be together and to talk about what's happening.

135
Don't allow the "silent treatment." Instead, talk it out.

136

Remember, everything takes longer than you think it will. Keep your spouse posted about delays, whether it's something that will make you late for dinner or the realization a home improvement project will take three years rather than the three weeks you first estimated.

137

Love means seeking what will benefit the other person.

138

Child-rearing years are stressful on a marriage.
Pay extra attention to your marriage
when you have small children.
Reserve time to be alone together.

139

Go together to a lecture, concert, or sports event
that your mate would especially enjoy.

140

When you find yourself thinking, *He or she* ought *to do . . .* , beware! Your mate will not necessarily react to or handle every event as you (or your parents) would. Talk about those little annoyances early. Discuss how you think things should be handled and decide together how to compromise.

141

Don't even *joke* about divorce or leaving.

142

Meet your spouse at the airport with a favorite treat,
balloons, and a warm hug.

143

Make an ongoing anniversary card to use year after
year. Each year, write a note about what has happened
during the past year together, date it, and sign it.
Reread all these notes together each anniversary.

144
Evening walks ease the tensions of the day
and help you get "reacquainted."

145
*"The happiness of married life depends upon making
small sacrifices with readiness and cheerfulness."*
—SELDEN

146

Surprises, even little ones, add suspense and excitement in a relationship. Plan a surprise today.

147

Don't let each other's spending become an issue. Try a cash budget using envelopes with ledgers for accountability.

148

Corrections and loving criticism always belong
in private—your mate needs your unconditional,
loving support in public.

149

Always focus on the wonderful things
about the unique personality of your spouse,
and remember your own imperfections
if you start thinking about his or hers.

150
Cultivate friendships with your in-laws.

151
Remember exactly what you promised
in your marriage vows.

152
None of us is perfect, but we will try
harder if we feel appreciated.

153

Don't hesitate to seek professional help
if you find that communication has broken down
between the two of you.

154

If your spouse is in a bad mood,
try not to take it personally.

155
Participate cheerfully in your mate's favorite activity
or hobby every once in a while, even if it isn't
the one you personally enjoy.

156
Plan a lazy Saturday. Stay in bed, read the newspaper,
bring fresh bagels and fruit for breakfast in bed.

157
Offer to cook and clean up after a meal
so your mate can have a "night off."

158
When you have a newborn, go out to dinner as
a couple at least by the time the baby is two months
old. You will need to remember where this family
began—with the *two* of you.

159
Don't worry about old flames. Don't bring up past relationships. You are the chosen one.

160
Work in the yard together, planting and cultivating, cleaning and repairing.

161
Avoid debt like the plague.

162
When you know the baby needs changing, do it.
Don't wait for your spouse to discover it.

———————◈———————

163
When you "sense" that there is a problem, there
probably is. Be gentle but persistent in drawing it out
in the open so that you can deal with it together.

164

Have a weekly "family staff meeting." (Try Sunday night after the kids are in bed.) Discuss your schedules for the coming week so you each know what to expect.

165

When you have the opportunity, give your mate the gift of a few extra minutes of sleep.

166
Start an investment of fifty dollars per month that is automatically taken out of your checking account and put into a mutual fund. It adds up quickly and can be used for a special purchase you otherwise could not afford.

167
Hug in bed for a few minutes every morning.

168
Use colored lights or candles in the bedroom to create
a romantic mood for special times together.

169
Have a planning weekend away without the kids
once every six months. Discuss long-term
and short-term family goals.

170

Take lots of pictures. They are tangible evidence of the history you have together. "Remember whens" are great for dissolving tension and reminding us why we are together and what we love about each other.

171

Take a class together. Try something new!
Auto mechanics, cooking, etc.

172

Agree beforehand, as much as you can, on how you want to raise your children and go forward together. When you are in the midst of a problem and find you are not in accord, take time to sort things out between the two of you, and not in front of the children.

173

Play footsie before you go to sleep each night.

174

Read magazines or books together and discuss them.

175

Find out what your spouse likes to do when she
comes in the door at the end of a work day. If she
needs fifteen minutes of peace and quiet, allow her
that, but if she wants to tell all about the day,
be an active listener.

176

Write your marital autobiography. Begin a journal
and set aside an hour each week or month to record
happy moments. Create your own "memoirs"
as you go along.

———————◈———————

177

Turn the alarm off and wake your
spouse with a back rub.

178
For anniversary or birthday gifts, give tickets
to events your spouse will enjoy.

❖

179
Even if you *can* do five things at once while listening
to your spouse, put everything down and look at him
while he is talking to you.

180

When you are both relaxed and in a pleasant mood,
ask the other, "If you could change one thing
about me, what would it be?"

181

Don't interrupt or correct when your mate
is telling a story or joke.

182
Give each other plenty of "space" to do your own thing.

183
Remember to be flexible. Our personal view
may not be the right or only one.

184
Don't argue in the heat of anger.
After you have calmed down, *then* talk.

185

Your mate can make love, make the bed, or make dinner, but he or she cannot make you happy. You must take that responsibility for yourself.

---◈---

186

Say what you mean, but don't "say it mean"!

---◈---

187

Write out a "memory list" of your favorite times together.

188
For your anniversary, write out new wedding
vows and exchange them each year.

189
Make a tape mix together of your favorite songs. Then
both of you can listen to them in the car or at home.

190
Reenact the scene of your engagement.

191
Make a magazine cut-out collage together
of pictures and phrases that make you laugh.

192
Turn the lights down and dance in the living room.

193
Each year plant a special perennial
to celebrate your anniversary.

194

Place a note where your spouse will see it early
in the day, saying that you are praying for him.

195

If business travel requires you to be apart for an
extended time, plan for both of you to read the same
thing while you are apart. Take notes for discussion
when you are together again.

196

Swim together under the stars. If you are in
a private place, forget the bathing suits.

———◉———

197

Surprise your spouse at work with a picnic lunch.

———◉———

198

Fight all feelings of self-pity, jealousy, and resentment.
They are destructive.

199
Remember: Love is spontaneous
but blossoms with discipline.

200
Watch your wedding video or look at your photos
together at least once a year.

201

Remember, everyone is exhausted at the end
of the day. Tiptoe around tired temperaments.

202

Work together in a soup kitchen or
a homeless shelter. It changes your
perspective on things.

203
Check with each other before accepting
social engagements.

◈

204
Cultivate the habit of separating at large parties
and receptions. It is fun when you get home to ask,
"Who did you talk to?"

205

Go to your mate's required functions with anticipation. You never know what interesting people you may meet.

206

Remember, no matter *how* strongly you feel, you could be wrong.

207
Even married people shouldn't let outside friendships
fall by the wayside. You will always need friends other
than your spouse.

208
Be open to your mate's ideas
even if you think you have a better answer.

209

Resist the temptation to make comparisons between
a hurtful action on the part of your spouse
with any painful thing you may have suffered
in a past relationship with someone else.

210

Leave each other love messages
on the answering machine.

211

When your mate travels, arrange for the hotel concierge to put a single rose by the bedside.

212

When driving on long trips, read interesting books or stories out loud to each other.

213

Mow "I love you" ("I ♥ U") in the grass.

214
Never underestimate the power of *chocolate*, to soothe wounds, make apologies, or encourage.

215
Do a chore that the other usually does, without being asked.

216
Invite your spouse out for a lunch date.

217
Write a "Top Ten Reasons I Love You"
list for your spouse.

◉

218
Have a "This Is Your Life" party to celebrate a big
birthday (thirty, forty, etc.). Ask friends from all over
to send letters you can put in a scrapbook.

219
Go back to the places you went
when you were dating.

220
Never try to discuss anything serious after 9:00 pm.

221
Give your mate a ten-second kiss when she comes in
the door at the end of the day.

222
Don't return gifts your spouse gives you.

223
In the beginning of your marriage, discuss your sexual relationship. Show your mate what pleases you and find out what pleases him or her.

224
Call home every night when you're traveling.

225

On winter mornings, clean the snow off his car
and turn on the heater before he goes outside.

226

Remember, "Blessed are they who can laugh at
themselves for they shall never cease to be amused."

227

A massage with hot oil and warm towels is always nice!

228
Think carefully before saying anything negative
about your mate's family or upbringing.
Casual insults of this nature are very painful.

229
Pretend you're in high school and go "parking"
after dark—kiss in the back seat of the car.

230
Attend a financial planning seminar together
and *use* what you learn.

———————◈———————

231
Write down your goals and talk about them together.
Think in terms of physical, mental, spiritual, social,
and emotional goals. Have your own but find some
to share, then work on getting there together.

232

Take candles with you when you travel together.
They add romance to a motel room.

233

Tell each other you look forward to spending time
together. Everyone needs to *hear* it said.

234

Turn off the television.

235
Cook dinner together.

236
"We never know how much one loves till we know how much he is willing to endure and suffer for us; and it is the suffering element that measures love."
—HENRY WARD BEECHER

237
Make love during the day before you're tired.

238
In a crowd, telegraph love to your spouse
across the room with your eyes.

239
Save up funny things that happen during the day
to share with each other in the evening.

240
Thank your spouse for doing a chore even if you feel like it *is* her job and not yours.

241
A kiss in the kitchen is worth ten in the bedroom.

242
Love never asks, "How much must I do?"
but "How much *can* I do?"

243
Before you flare up at your mate's faults, take time to count to ten—ten of your own!

244
Give each other silly toys just for fun.

245
Never cease to be alert to something you can honestly praise in your spouse—and do it often.

246
Don't leave the house without
kissing each other goodbye.

247
Whenever possible, spend the day together on your
birthdays. Money need not be spent—just celebrate
the birth of your very special someone.

248
Find new spots in your home to make love.

249
Compliment, affirm, and encourage your spouse
often in front of your children.

250
Keep your bedroom attractive—a haven
just for the two of you.

251

Tell each other what you "need." No one can read minds or know where the other's "itch" is. If you don't verbalize them, you may act out your needs in less appropriate ways.

252

Have family "laugh-ins"—times when you roll around on the floor, act silly, and see who can be the goofiest. Encourage your children to join in.

253
Rake leaves together into a big pile, bury each other,
and have leaf wars. Invite the kids to join in!

254
Put the kids to bed early, order carry-out, dress
up in "nothings" and enjoy each other's
presence over dinner.

255
Play strip poker together! (No fair putting on extra layers of clothes before the game starts!)

256
When you have children, put a lock on your bedroom door. Use it.

257
Sleep in front of a roaring fire.

258

"Hear" your mate without giving solutions or moralizing too quickly. Give him or her room to arrive at a personal resolution of an issue while experiencing your support.

259

Take a trip together to show your spouse favorite places from your childhood.

260

When telling your spouse something difficult, remember to communicate affection with body language. Touch the arm, take the hand, stroke the cheek . . . something to remind him that he is loved regardless of the difficult issue at hand.

261

Plan a surprise scavenger hunt for your mate. Be the final prize in a hidden place.

262

Don't meet with a person
of the opposite sex in private.
Leave office doors open, or use glass doors.

263

Have a pillow fight or tickling
session with your spouse.

264

Design your imaginary "dream home" together.
It may never become a reality, but dreaming
together is free and fun.

---◈---

265

Read the Song of Songs (also called the Song of
Solomon) from the Bible out loud to your mate.

266

Ask your in-laws for childhood photos of your mate
and put them in a special album for him or her.

———————————◆———————————

267

Appreciate the different backgrounds and customs
each of you brings into your marriage. They are meant
to enrich your life together.

268

Go for a brisk walk alone to blow off steam
before you confront your mate.

269

Have a "Two-Dollar Date." Go to a local mall
and see how far you can stretch two dollars—
you might be surprised.

270

Place objects that have a special message or will evoke
a memory where your mate will discover them.
For example, a matchbook cover from a favorite
restaurant, a theater ticket, etc.

271

Balance the checkbook monthly and be sure you both
know the balance and where the money is going.

272
Talk over your "division of labor"
on a regular basis.

273
Communication is not just conveying information.
It means two-way conversation until the meaning
of the message is clear.

274
If you're the first one to wake up in the morning,
empty the dishwasher.

275
Chart your family histories together.
Learn your genealogy.

276
Start a new collection together.

277
Put a photo of each of your childhood
homes together in a frame.

278
When you're at the beach,
write a message, send it out in a bottle
with your name and phone number,
then wait and see what happens.

279

Play sardines in the dark with your children.
One person hides, everyone else "seeks," and whoever
finds the hiding person, hides with them!

280

Write your spouse your "last love letter,"
including all the things you've never said
but meant to.

281

Keep this in mind in difficult times:
"*If God is going to do something wonderful, he starts with a problem. If God is going to do something spectacular, he starts with an impossibility.*"

—ANONYMOUS

282

Write the story of how you fell in love to read to your children someday.

283

Make sure you both have a clear knowledge of where your will is, what your life insurance policies are, and have made arrangements for the care of your children *just in case*.

284

Sing to your mate.

285

"Adopt" a needy family at Thanksgiving and at Christmas. Take the holiday meal and presents to them.

286

Avoid offering unsolicited advice to your spouse.

287

"What greater thing is there for two souls
than to feel that they are joined for life—
to strengthen each other in all labor,
to rest on each other in all sorrow,
to minister to each other in all pain,
to be one with each other in silent, unspeakable memories
at the moment of the last parting."

—GEORGE ELIOT

Especially For Him

288
Spend time with other men who love their wives
and talk about them in a positive way.

289
When your wife is exhausted at the end of the day,
take her in your arms and simply tell her
how wonderful she is.

290
Learn what she does at work and who her friends are.

291
Make sure she doesn't run out of perfume.

292
Clothes *beside* the hamper are certainly an effort,
but go for the dunk!

293
Don't expect her to be like your mom.

294
Bring her flowers just because.

295
Tell your children they have the best mom
in the world.

296
Learn her cycle and grant her extra grace if she has PMS. Don't take what she says too personally.

———————◈———————

297
Hug her in front of the kids.

———————◈———————

298
If it plugs in, don't give it to her for her birthday, anniversary, or Christmas.

299
When she's upset about something she may not need your solution. Instead, hold her and tell her that you understand.

300
Tell her she's sexy. Tell her again and again, especially if you've been married a long time.

301
When she is trying to get your attention,
stop what you are doing and give it to her.

302
Imagine that you are not yet married to her,
but still dating. What is some romantic little thing
you might have done for her? Do it today.

303
Make the bed in the morning while she's in the shower.

304
Initiate a back massage for her every so often
(without the expectation of sex).

305
Offer to invite her favorite friend or relative for a visit.

306
Do at least one thing for her each day,
without being asked.

307
When she's crabby don't criticize her.
Encourage her instead.

308
Mail her a card telling her you love her.

309
Listen to what she is feeling
as well as what she is saying.
Respond from your heart, not just your head.

———————◆———————

310
Ask her advice about a decision you are wrestling
with. Let her know that what she thinks is
important to you.

311
Tell her something nice you've thought about her
this week but haven't put into words.

312
Give her a love note, poem, or a small gift
on the monthly anniversary of your wedding.

313
Help the children fix breakfast in bed for her.

314
You *can* do things like shopping, cleaning, vacuuming,
laundry, cooking. . . . Do them!

315
If she says you've hurt her feelings, say "I'm sorry,"
not "Why would that hurt your feelings?"
or "I didn't do it on purpose."

316
Carry her over the threshold into your new home each time you move.

317
Fill up her gas tank for her.

318
Open doors for her.

319

Declare a Mother's Day in January.
Treat her like a queen.
Take the kids, clean the house,
and send her out for the day.

320

Arrange baby-sitting and kidnap her
for an overnight stay in a hotel.

321
Tell her she's lovely when she feels ugly. Tell her again.

322
Hug your wife before you hug the kids when you come home. They need to know Mom is first.

323
If she's making the bed or folding laundry, go to her and help—she'll feel encouraged.

324
Buy her a sexy nightgown.

325
Thank her for dinner every night and teach
your children to do the same.

326
Put the toilet lid down.

327
When she looks pretty, tell her so.
Don't just think it.

328
Don't ever allow the children to talk back
to her. Instead insist they treat her with respect.
Always.

329

Be every bit as quick to respond to her requests—
whatever they may be—when you have been
married for a long time as you were when you
were just falling in love.

ESPECIALLY FOR HER

330

Spend time with other women who love their husbands and who encourage you to love yours better.

———◈———

331

Tell your husband why you are sad or upset. Don't expect him to be a mind reader.

332
Tell him you're proud of his accomplishments at work.

———————◆———————

333
Always build him up to the children.
Never cut him down.

———————◆———————

334
Write him a note telling him what you
admire about him.

335

Put a note on the outside door telling him to follow the candles to find you. Set candles out leading to wherever you'll be. Just before he arrives, light the candles and put his favorite music on.
Note: This requires good timing.

336

He probably *is* lost. Try to help find directions while protecting his male ego.

337
Remember, he comes before the children.
Make time to be with just him.

338
Upgrade your lingerie.

339
Tell him you admire his brains but you love his body.

340
Tell the kids three things you love about their dad.

341
Affirm one of his strengths. Tell him something you think he's good at.

342
Remember, inside the man is a little boy.

343
Encourage the kids to write him love notes.

344
Seduce him.

345
Don't expect him to be like your dad.

346
Let your man be a man.
Don't expect him to respond like a female.

347
Vacuum his car.

348
Give him the gift of time with his friends.

349
Write a love poem for him.

350
Sew missing buttons on his shirts.

351
Give him ample warning when "that time of the month" is coming, so he will understand the reason if your moods change.

352

Never correct or reprimand him in public.

353

Give him some quiet time every day to read
the newspaper or his favorite magazine.
Teach the kids to respect his alone time.

354

Kiss the back of his neck when he's sitting at his desk.

355
Ask your mother-in-law for one of your husband's
favorite childhood recipes, and prepare it
for him as a surprise.

356
Have his business colleagues to dinner.

357
Buy him a toy, like a squirt gun.

358

Don't let yourself get lazy about your appearance. Suppose you had not met until thirty years after the wedding—would he still ask you for a date?

359

Feed the kids early, fix his favorite meal, and serve it in front of a roaring fire.

360
Compliment him in front of others.

361
Don't hit him with a big discussion
right when he walks in the door.

362
Kidnap him after work one day
and go to a hotel for an overnight.

363
Fix his favorite breakfast and serve it to him in bed.

364
Initiate sex when he isn't expecting it. For example,
when you both wake up in the middle of the night,
early in the morning, etc.

365
Write a love message with soap on his shower wall.

*"If you treat a man as he is, he will stay as he is.
But if you treat him as if he were what he ought to be,
and could be, he will become
a bigger and better man."*

—GOETHE

HELP US KEEP *Tightening* THE KNOT!

Do you have ideas or insights you've "couple-tested" in your own marriage that you think would be helpful to others?

**If you do, we'd like to hear about them!
Send your top three ideas, name, city and state, and
(if you choose) how long you've been married to:**

Allison Yates Gaskins
**c/o Piñon Press
P.O. Box 35007
Colorado Springs, CO 80935**

**If we get enough great responses, we may publish them—
along with each contributor's first name and other information—
in a second volume of *Tightening the Knot*.**

All responses become the property of Susan Alexander Yates and Allison Yates Gaskins and
may be published without further permission of sender.

Other books by Susan Alexander Yates:

And Then I Had Kids: Encouragement for Mothers of Young Children
    (Word Publishing, 1988)
A House Full of Friends, Building Intimate Relationships within Your Family
    (Focus on the Family Publishing, 1995)

By John and Susan Yates:

*What Really Matters at Home: Eight Crucial Elements for Building Character in
    Your Family* (Word Publishing, 1992)